Legacy Youth Journal

Boys and Young Men of Color

Dear Scholar:

I hope that you find this journal useful, friendly, and inspiring as you continue to strive to new heights.

Journaling is important when crafting your voice. I learned how to journal in middle school. It helps to safely look back at my struggles and to celebrate my accomplishments and those dear to me.

If you have never journaled before, I want to ask you to start with finding time and a quiet space. Be open and honest with your reflections and trust the process.

If you'd like a little boost to get started, search YouTube for "The Dr. Selma B. Show." You'll see how I integrate journaling with short confidence-boosting videos to advocate for you.

As an educator, I advocate for different learning styles. A journal doesn't have to be in writing. The questions in this journal offer a structure. If you feel like you are not ready to write every day or weekly, then I encourage you to use a voice recorder or complete a video journal to answer the questions. What matters most is that you engage in the journaling process. Trust ... and you will hone your voice.

The pages of our day seem to always be always filled. A blank page gives you your power back and allows you to claim your breakthrough. You can do this! You can write caring, open, and meaningful reflections. I hope you'll complete this guide and have it as a product that you can constantly refer to. Scholar ... use it until it becomes dog-eared and stained with your hopes.

Dream Big and Have Fun!

Dr. Selma K. Bartholomew "Dr. B."
President
PartnerWithLegacy

How to Use this Journal Guide

 Watch The Dr. Selma B. Show
Stop Doing and Start Achieving

 Make time to reflect and complete your journal.

 Practice being openminded and put the words in your heart on the pages.

 You may also record your answers to the journal questions.

 You may also complete a video journal. What matters is working through the process of reflecting.

About The Legacy Youth Journal: Boys and Young Men of Color

The Legacy Youth Journal is focused on helping you hone your voice and build your confidence. It is a journal that you can complete independently or with a teacher or mentor who is helping to guide and support you on your path towards your goal.

The Legacy Youth Journal journal was developed with the hope of calling your attention to a national and international community of leaders, educators, and change agents who are actively working to help change outcomes for young people. The goal is to let you know that you—as a young scholar—are not alone and that there are people all over the globe fighting and cheering for your success.

Here's a little background for you: President Barack Hussein Obama became the first African-American male to become president in 2008. As president he successfully passed the Affordable Care Act, which helped provide health care for more than 20 million Americans. He also rescued the economy when he signed a 787-billion-dollar American Recovery and Reinvestment Act in 2009, which served to kickstart economic growth amid the most severe economic downturn since the Great Depression.

During his presidency he had to deal with many national conflicts that tested his leadership. In February 2012, the world was shocked by the killing of Trayvon Martin. Trayvon Benjamin Martin was only 17 years when he taken from this earth. He was a young man who loved music, played football as a young kid, and volunteered in his community. His memory lives on and the promise of his future is wrapped up in the hopes and dreams of ALL young people.

In 2014, President Obama set a plan in motion to change the narrative. The My Brother's Keeper initiative was launched to address persistent opportunity gaps facing boys and young men of color and to ensure that all youth can reach their full potential. This initiative grew and in 2015 it became the My Brother's Keeper Alliance (MBK Alliance) and then in 2017 the MBK Alliance initiative became part of the Obama Foundation.

The MBK Alliance is a national call to action that is focused on building safe and supportive communities for Boys and Young Men of Color where they feel valued and have clear pathways to opportunity. We also recognize that Girls of Color face similar challenges.

PartnerWithLegacy's work as a company is to help educators create classrooms that are more engaging and supportive for each and every child. We are inspired by the MBK Alliance's work and seek to answer that call to action. This journal is our response to a need that we recognized while working with our teachers and scholars. We wanted to create space where you as a scholar would be encouraged to tell your story and learn how to reflect on all that is happening in your life and the world around you. That space is within the journal pages. We created this tool to help more of our young people stay on track, understand their value, and organize their thoughts and goals to make positive change. Use it to make your hopes and dreams come true.

My Brother's Keeper Alliance Milestones

Learn More:

- **Getting a Healthy Start and Entering School Ready to Learn**
  *All children should have a healthy start and enter school ready —
  cognitively, physically, socially, and emotionally.*

- **Reading at Grade Level by Third Grade**
  *All children should be reading at grade level by age 8 — the age at
  which reading to learn becomes essential.*

- **Graduating from High School Ready for College and Career**
  *All youth should receive a quality high school education
  and graduate with the skills and tools needed to advance to
  postsecondary education or training.*

- **Completing Postsecondary Education or Training**
  *Every American should have the option to attend postsecondary
  education and receive the education and training needed for the
  quality jobs of today and tomorrow.*

- **Successfully Entering the Workforce**
  *Anyone who wants a job should be able to get a job that allows
  them to support themselves and their families.*

- **Keeping Kids on Track and Giving Them Second Chances**
  *All youth and young adults should be safe from violent crime; and
  individuals who are confined should receive the education, training,
  and treatment they need for a second chance.*

99 *You may not always have a comfortable life and you will not always be able to solve all of the world's problems at once. But, don't ever underestimate the importance you can have because history has shown us that courage can be contagious, and hope can take on a life of its own.*
—Mrs. Michelle Obama

99 *THAT'S WHAT 'MY BROTHER'S KEEPER' IS ALL ABOUT.*
Helping more of our young people stay on track. Providing the support they need to think more broadly about their future. Building on what works—when it works, in those critical life—changing moments.
—President Barack Obama

Remarks by President Obama on Trayvon Martin (July 19, 2013)

Read the text of the speech or watch the video of the speech given by President Obama about Trayvon Martin. After you read or watch the speech, think about your reaction to it. Use the "Quote, Note or Thought" organizer to put your thoughts and reactions into words.

How did the speech challenge your thinking—or inspire you in any way?

Quotes, Notes, Warm and Cool Thoughts

Text: Remarks by President Obama on Trayvon Martin (July 19, 2013)

Quotes	Notes	Warm and Cool Thoughts
The author said...	I think this is important to remember ...	I liked... I wondered if... I'm still questioning... I valued... I can't justify...

Journaling Sentence Starters

I love it when I …

I won't ever stop until I….

I will keep focus and trying..

I want to improve on ….

I love it when I..

Mistakes help me …

I am going to be known for …

What happened today made me...

I can learn from this...

I think the best way to solve...

I try really hard …

Legacy Youth Journal: Boys and Young Men of Color

Day 1

President Barack Obama was the first black person to be elected president in the United States. In 2020, Kamala Harris became the first woman and person of color to be elected Vice President. Do you have a first that you are proud of? As you look ahead, is there a first that you would like to achieve?

Legacy Youth Journal: Boys and Young Men of Color

✌

Day 2

The tragic death of Mr. George Floyd in 2020 uplifted the Black Lives Matter movement (BLM) and the push for justice and equality. What are your questions and concerns about George Floyd's death? What impact has the BLM movement had on your thinking about yourself?

Legacy Youth Journal: Boys and Young Men of Color

❧

Day 3

What quote from President Obama's speech about Travvon Martin is the most important to you? Why?

Legacy Youth Journal: Boys and Young Men of Color

Day 4

How do you think your life has been easy or difficult? Why?

Legacy Youth Journal: Boys and Young Men of Color

Day 5

What change do you want to create in the world?
What are you passionate about?

Legacy Youth Journal: Boys and Young Men of Color

Day 6

What do you need to do to reach your goal? Who could you ask for help?

Legacy Youth Journal: Boys and Young Men of Color

❧

Day 7

It is essential to know what we do well and to recognize our strengths. What are your strengths?

Legacy Youth Journal: Boys and Young Men of Color

Day 8

What qualities would your best friend say they admire most about you? What makes you a good friend? Or A good 'Brother"?

Legacy Youth Journal:
Boys and Young Men of Color

Day 9

*What does it mean to you to be a
Young Man of Color?*

Legacy Youth Journal: Boys and Young Men of Color

❧

Day 10

*Have you ever failed at something?
What did you learn about that failure?*

Legacy Youth Journal: Boys and Young Men of Color

⁂

Day 11

How do you go about choosing your friends?

Legacy Youth Journal: Boys and Young Men of Color

❧

Day 12

If you could be granted three wishes for someone you love, what would you wish for and why?

Legacy Youth Journal: Boys and Young Men of Color

⚬

Day 13

What kinds of things do you enjoy doing,
and what are you curious about?

Legacy Youth Journal: Boys and Young Men of Color

Day 14

How do you go about resolving conflict?

Legacy Youth Journal: Boys and Young Men of Color

❧

Day 15

How do you show respect and care for "Sisters"?
How do you show respect and care for "Brothers"?

Legacy Youth Journal: Boys and Young Men of Color

∼

Day 16

What questions do you have about your future?

Legacy Youth Journal:
Boys and Young Men of Color

≈

Day 17

*What do you think you want to do
after high school?*

Legacy Youth Journal: Boys and Young Men of Color

⤜⤛

Day 18

What do you know about college life?
What do you want to know about college life?

Legacy Youth Journal: Boys and Young Men of Color

Day 19

Write or sketch about anything here that you'd like: frustrations, hopes, or dreams.

Legacy Youth Journal: Boys and Young Men of Color

Day 20

As a result of journaling, what have you learned about yourself?

Legacy Youth Journal: Boys and Young Men of Color Stop Doing and Start Achieving

Strategic, Measurable, Attainable, Realistic, and Timely (SMART) Goals.
What are you seeking to achieve?

Priorities: What must you focus on to get to your goals?
1. _____
2. _____
3. _____
4. _____
5. _____

To Do List: Handling the small things once will help you gain and keep your momentum. You will be amazed at how quickly you get to your goals and priorities.
1. _____
2. _____
3. _____
4. _____
5. _____

Legacy Youth Journal: Boys and Young Men of Color Stop Doing and Start Achieving

Strategic, Measurable, Attainable, Realistic, and Timely (SMART) Goals.
What are you seeking to achieve?

Priorities: What must you focus on to get to your goals?
1. _____
2. _____
3. _____
4. _____
5. _____

To Do List: Handling the small things once will help you gain and keep your momentum. You will be amazed at how quickly you get to your goals and priorities.
1. _____
2. _____
3. _____
4. _____
5. _____

Legacy Youth Journal: Boys and Young Men of Color Stop Doing and Start Achieving

Strategic, Measurable, Attainable, Realistic, and Timely (SMART) Goals.
What are you seeking to achieve?

Priorities: What must you focus on to get to your goals?
1. _____
2. _____
3. _____
4. _____
5. _____

To Do List: Handling the small things once will help you gain and keep your momentum. You will be amazed at how quickly you get to your goals and priorities.
1. _____
2. _____
3. _____
4. _____
5. _____

Legacy Youth Journal: Boys and Young Men of Color Stop Doing and Start Achieving

Strategic, Measurable, Attainable, Realistic, and Timely (SMART) Goals.
What are you seeking to achieve?

Priorities: What must you focus on to get to your goals?
1. _____
2. _____
3. _____
4. _____
5. _____

To Do List: Handling the small things once will help you gain and keep your momentum. You will be amazed at how quickly you get to your goals and priorities.
1. _____
2. _____
3. _____
4. _____
5. _____

Legacy Youth Journal: Boys and Young Men of Color Stop Doing and Start Achieving

Strategic, Measurable, Attainable, Realistic, and Timely (SMART) Goals.
What are you seeking to achieve?

Priorities: What must you focus on to get to your goals?
1. _____
2. _____
3. _____
4. _____
5. _____

To Do List: Handling the small things once will help you gain and keep your momentum. You will be amazed at how quickly you get to your goals and priorities.
1. _____
2. _____
3. _____
4. _____
5. _____

Legacy Youth Journal: Boys and Young Men of Color Stop Doing and Start Achieving

Strategic, Measurable, Attainable, Realistic, and Timely (SMART) Goals.
What are you seeking to achieve?

Priorities: What must you focus on to get to your goals?
1. _____
2. _____
3. _____
4. _____
5. _____

To Do List: Handling the small things once will help you gain and keep your momentum. You will be amazed at how quickly you get to your goals and priorities.
1. _____
2. _____
3. _____
4. _____
5. _____

Legacy Youth Journal: Boys and Young Men of Color Stop Doing and Start Achieving

Strategic, Measurable, Attainable, Realistic, and Timely (SMART) Goals.
What are you seeking to achieve?

Priorities: What must you focus on to get to your goals?
1. _____
2. _____
3. _____
4. _____
5. _____

To Do List: Handling the small things once will help you gain and keep your momentum. You will be amazed at how quickly you get to your goals and priorities.
1. _____
2. _____
3. _____
4. _____
5. _____

Legacy Youth Journal: Boys and Young Men of Color Stop Doing and Start Achieving

Strategic, Measurable, Attainable, Realistic, and Timely (SMART) Goals.
What are you seeking to achieve?

Priorities: What must you focus on to get to your goals?
1. _____
2. _____
3. _____
4. _____
5. _____

To Do List: Handling the small things once will help you gain and keep your momentum. You will be amazed at how quickly you get to your goals and priorities.
1. _____
2. _____
3. _____
4. _____
5. _____

Continue to Craft
the Inner Warrior Within.

Check Out Our
Warrior Journal Series
Available on Amazon

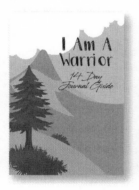

Get Inspired

*Join Our
Community of Warriors.
Subscribe Today and
Get for Free Our*

Inspiration
Warrior:

Introduction Journal Guide

*PartnerWithLegacy
Home of*

THE
DR. SELMA B
Show

About The Author

Dr. Selma K. Bartholomew, known as Dr. B., for more than 25 years, has worked to improve educational outcomes for children and families. She began her career teaching mathematics at Lehman College in the Bronx, taught math and physics at Jacqueline Kennedy Onassis High School in NY, students in group homes, women in prison, and in Fordham University's Graduate School of Education. In 2008, she stepped out on faith and founded her company PartnerWithLegacy to help schools become a place of purpose, passion, and innovation. PartnerWithLegacy's work in STEM is transformative and rests on the theory of learning that Math is a Language.

Dr. B's love for journaling and writing was cultivated growing up in Harlem and spending hours after school getting lost in books at the famous Countee Cullen and Arturo Schomburg Library. Her goal is to inspire and motivate writers and readers (of ALL ages) to find their voice and fight for their passion. Connect with her to learn more about the work of her company, team and mission. Get inspired by visiting PartnerWithLegacy's YouTube channel— Home of The Dr. Selma B. Show.

Made in the USA
Middletown, DE
27 September 2021